Sea of Rocks

By
Lucía Orellana-Damacela

Sea of Rocks

By
Lucía Orellana-Damacela

Copyright © Lucía Orellana-Damacela 2018.
All rights reserved.

No part of this book may be reproduced in any form whatsoever without the written consent of Unsolicited Press (except for brief quotations in critical articles or reviews and in non-commercial uses permitted by copyright law).

Cover and interior design by Nicholas Morrison
Edited by Kristen Gustafson

ISBN: 978-1-947021-72-3

Published by Unsolicited Press
www.unsolicitedpress.com
Portland, OR 97239
(619) 354-8005

Unsolicited Press books are distributed to the trade by Ingram.

Attention schools and businesses: Discount copies are available for bulk orders. Please contact our team at orders@unsolicitedpress.com.

Contents

***

Insomnia	13
You Again	14
The Angel in My Cupboard	15
Looking Up	17
Ice Love	19
Fireworks	21
Night in Akumal	22
Sound Proof	24
Density	25
Staycation	26
Planned Giving	28

***

Road Map	31
The Fall	32
Undertones	33
Street Art	34
Drift	35
Leftovers	37
Passing by Some Minor Ruins on Our Way to Chichen Itza	38
Portrait	39

Thirst	40
Fallen Lights	41
Memory Shipwreck	42

***

Winter Night	45
Bleeding Rocks	46
Hanging On	47
Unseen	48
Partition of the Waters	50
Celebration	51
Sett Patterns	52
Inkception	54
Coalescence	56
Along the Ocean	58
Notes	61
Acknowledgements	62

To Roque, Roque Darío, and Gabriela

Sea of Rocks

By
Lucía Orellana-Damacela

***

Insomnia

One by one,
sheep fall down the cliff

after jumping the fence
I built to save them.

The potpourri's aroma
—charming in the evening—

becomes effluvium
at three in the morning.

The glass of warm milk,
rancid aftertaste of the day.

So I sleepwalk
Borges' Labyrinths.

You Again

Your face on the lagoon, not a reflection,
rather an encounter of sorts.
You look pale, washed out,
not quite belonging,
like the moon at sunset;
a blister on bruised sky,
broken into waves;
your voice lost, eaten by fish.

In my nightmares,
you are the one who counted
seventeen, sixteen, fifteen,
and couldn't find me at one.
Only the moon was there,
a garlic clove, a failed charm.

And then I wake up.
I always wake up.

The Angel in My Cupboard

The angel living in my cupboard
doesn't flaunt angel hair
his mane looks rather like
a spoonful of whipped cream cheese

the angel hiding in my cupboard
is most visible when the evening light
penetrates the room through
the sealed high window

the angel squatting in my cupboard
dresses with the dust that flies off
the rice bags
and has snout beetles for breakfast

the angel lying down in my cupboard
asks me for help to fix his broken wings
but none of the materials he lists
are available on Amazon

the angel stiffening in my cupboard
flaps his wings as if conjuring
Prometheus and Icarus
to no avail

the angel in my cupboard
formerly crafted of light and specks
is becoming solid as rock
except rocks don't cry.

Looking Up

You are that story
I blurt

when the lights are out
and I can't see the mirrors.

The few memory crumbs I keep
are not enough to recreate you.

What else is left? The shades
you wore to eclipse your eyes.

The photo of the adopted cat
that abandoned you years ago.

Undone To-do lists written
with the astronaut's pen you used…

which, by the way,
was mine first;

you borrowed
and never returned it.

But you need it more than I do
because in my story

you are in space
looking at me,

thinking of me,
perhaps writing me a letter.

Ice Love

A man and a woman
Play at being strangers

They stand in front of each other
The woman holds a square sheet of ice
She moves slightly forward
Hands the ice to the man
Who moves slightly forward
Passes it to the woman
And so forth   their nails white from exposure
Trembling with thermal overload
When holding the ice
Their fingers red
With desire   pulsating   for ice
When waiting for it

Ice can take their warmth no more
And they end empty-handed
Cold puddles around their naked feet
Unsettled islands
They are almost touching
Body heat invades each other's space
Hearts regain their rhythm
Embodied memory of ice
A tingle in their hands

How is it   they may ask
That this feels so much like fire?

Fireworks

Gazes peer through
haze-coated clouds

and capture exploding
bouquets

Your hand touches mine
and transforms my skin and my spine

into conductors of the power that flows
between the guarded reflective

amnesic sand
and the world that above us

dissolves in light.

Night in Akumal

A total blackout irrupted
into our dinner on the deck
by the beach.

The moon, uninvested,
left the scene.

The ocean, liquid drumming
accompanying the wind's voice.

      Our contours erased.

By touch, we found each other;
the salty glow
of our thirst our beacon.

      And the stars.

That velvet shield with silver sequins,
rhinestones   astral crystals,
   luminescent tacks
that hold on the dark board of the night.

That night that threw all its jacks
on the black mantle.

Our whispering words.

Fireflies in the roaring darkness,
guided us home.

Sound Proof

Surround-sound construction,
hydraulic hammers jamming
with dump trucks and compactors.
Heavy metal open ground concert
from dawn to dusk.

Echoes bounce off the walls,
a million vinyl empty tracks
crackle in an endless loop.
The robust, steady rhythm
of your blood running to meet me
dampens the intruder's roar.

We overpower it with the pop
and the fizz of the sparkling
you have poured for brunch;
bubbles in my mouth,
I ride the crest of the high decibels.

Density

The smell of euphony
Hibiscus scent
Captured by a solar panel
Released by a windmill

The harnessing of something bigger
Than myself and my confines
A density that tastes
Like your sweat at sunset

Staycation

It is summer
and both of us are between jobs.
My sister calls;
they are going to Margarita Island, she says.
That is the place where Simon Bolivar
started his independence quest
that freed five countries
I think, but don't mention.

Nor do I tell her my plans;
for us, a tent in the yard will do.
I am counting on stars, candles, and body heat
for entertainment;
we got rid of cable two weeks ago.

Our bounty
consists of a bag of wild rice and a few cans.
I pulse for more and find some lentils.

Lotus-seated, we share the last remains
with a beer and fresh salad;
the squeezed moon provides the dressing.

The moment is broken by the ring of my phone;
I get the waited call.

Oppression or liberation,
I am not sure,
but tomorrow will be Monday again.

Planned Giving

"I love you to bits," she said.
(Mind you, it was not me).

Well, that sounds intense, he thought,
"let's give it a try," he said.
(Mind you, it was not him).

But it was not meant to be.
The bits of him she craved the most
were the ones he intended to keep.

***

Road Map

A weary rhythm
in our conversation
white noise masking our voices
followed by blind spots of silence
passengers on a set course
that hauls us
farther away
dodging questions
      road hazards
cordoning off answers
      encasing the openness
the sycamores out there
      flanking sweeping fields
as we drive by
      fastened with words
leaving behind fences
      but not really
my heart's at stake
      that stake or perhaps that one
can't grasp it
      we pass by too fast
while Springsteen
      tags along.

The Fall

I drive down the hill
overlooking the ocean
coasting at full speed
roof top retracted
wind dread locking my hair
with the smell of raw salt

Always a narrator never the hero
gets to you   tires you
makes you want to leave everything behind
and just feel for once   just feel

For what it's worth
I don't care what happens
when I reach the main road
Right now my face is redder than
the roses bunched in the front gardens

Forever cautious I hit the brakes on time
turn right and follow the procession
Things will be uphill when I return.

Undertones

My texts to you accumulate
on my screen
one after the other,
uninterrupted threads of silence,
ties on an abandoned railroad.

My knocks on your door
resonate in the empty hallway
with the sound of cracking
stone-like eggs
of a mythical half human,
half rock-bottom creature.

At the end of your voyage
from the blue depths,
this shore awaits
where living beings of your species
go about their daily business.

I am here,
sunglasses in hand,
to fight the glare together.

Street Art

Windows
from
office
buildings
mining
the
sun
light
drawing
iridescent
lines
spectra
on
the
pavement
mother-of-pearl shells
flattened disco balls

I stepped on them
as I passed by

I wish I had stopped and danced

Drift

Sky cubes in my coffee,
I stretch within my shoes
inside my stiff,
perfectly ironed suit
hidden under my coat;
body mask from this year's collection.

Your postcard,
a sunshine spread on my dining table.

The urge I deemed extinguished
reddens my pale cheeks.
The shore is far from calm
and waves still obey the moon.

The plight
that almost drowned you,
your rocky start,
your saline solutions;
all come back to me.

Your deconstructed life
dictated by tide,
hopping from this island
to another.

Not that this matters, really.
Just say the word
and I'll swim the invisible current
that connects our two wrecks.

Leftovers

I put on my maple-colored coat, and a holdover
emerges from my pocket: the *Phantom of the Opera*
ticket stub from when we did touristy things.

My to-do list adrenaline rush is briefly halted;
the nonsense of an ending whispers itself back
to life, takes hold of the room barely reached
by a sun still getting out of the sheets.

When was the last time I felt you with this sense
of anticipation? As if I am late to our encounter
at the usual coffee shop, blue awning and a view
of the High Line. Where your blunt coming clean
chilled my cup of java. Where I poured coffee down
your trousers, hoping its stain had longer staying power
than me.

My heart still skips a beat too often, like when I see
the home delivery sign we laughed about —which
announces with unfortunate letter spacing that goods
are just *a click away*— and indulge in the afterthought
that so are you.

And here I am again, wondering how it could be
that you took off your mask and I became the ghost.

Passing by Some Minor Ruins on Our Way to Chichen Itza

Sounds
        captured within a chamber
        that no longer exists
a slightly harder type of soil
        more compact
        somewhat more put together
remnants that have forgotten
less about themselves
        about their shape
        about the shadows they
        projected over the side road.

A dead wall
a container for
a certain routine
        A sacrifice chamber perhaps?
        Or a room to welcome
        the new lives?

Everybody in town knew
but they are also dust now.

Portrait

The incandescent click doesn't reach you;
you, who moved out of the picture,
photobombing with your absence.

Thirst

Spaces left by ghosts of other spaces   waves
not reflecting but fizzing the moon
like an old-fashioned Alka Seltzer

If I dig   sometimes   I find water underneath
a ghost puddle   out of place
rain engorges it   hear it from my window
          The rattling rocking the boats
          floating on the light-turquoise fabric
          against the dark behind the glass

The rain is slowing down now
          while waiting for the other shoe to drop
          But that won't happen
          there isn't another foot
          except for the six ones under which
          I buried my grief

What is left of you may find its way
          resurfacing through that puddle
You shouldn't bother   really   You are
always here   in the water I drink
and in the one I don't
          A thirsty presence.

Fallen Lights

Turning the corner of the road
where my office sits, I reminded myself
to save the impression of how summer
sunset light goes to church
through the stained-glass windows,
and then regurgitates some glow
into my soul and onto the pavement.

Yellows, purples, violets, blues,
crushed under my sole.
A one-dimensional bouquet that reverberates
through my feet
and I can't bring home with me.

Except for this transubstantiated version
I captured today.

Memory Shipwreck

There are no more traces
of summer evenings in the garden,
of half-full glasses of wine,
of rugs faded with the weight
of lonely outings,
of waking up with the taste
of rancid oblivion in the tongue,
of the white contours of the pillow
molded with abandonment,
of rains that flooded the basement
and carried away your letters and my pictures.

And then we stopped tossing ropes to one another
trying to survive together the shipwreck.
Instead, each one made its own raft with the debris
and drifted with the current
toward steady shores,
toward new scents and newer promises.
But the memories we crafted
still lurk in the deepest and darkest bottom
of the waters.

***

Winter Night

I lie flat in the snow, a fallen angel
with beads of crystal on its face.

Buried up to my cheeks, the sounds
from the highway and from the wind

slapping the trees that circle
the church reverberate in my brain,

remixed as muffled *om* chanting.
The cadences in my body unhurried,

I become weightless.
The darkness above, barely pierced

by bullets of light,
mirrors the shadows that surround me.

That black canopy almost envelops
me now. It is so close that I can cloud it

with my breath.
The midnight chimes call me back.

Armored in cold resolve,
my words my sword, I carry on.

Bleeding Rocks

Garden stones after a rainstorm,
smooth and polished as empty words.
Beneath one, forgotten nuts and bolts,
a rusty nail. Puddles of dead metal blood.

Under the light drizzle, the call of the ink.
I dip my finger into this ochre well,
draw some wishes on a rock's surface
and then on the next one and so forth.

My wishes soon wash off. Unable
to impress unyielding stones, I turn
to the task at hand. As a matter of choice,
I could build a path or could erect a wall.

Hanging On

The long black coat hangs in the armoire
        heavy with silence
decades of un-wornness
a lifetime in the tropics
gathered in the seams

Dead at eighty six
she never returned
to her woolen-some place

        Or did she?

Bed-ridden for a year
what if once set free
        she flew
to the brown green mountains
her eyes took the color from
saw the intact   unclouded   un-cataracted
blue sky?

Better than imagining grandma's
soft stare hanging on forever
within some colorless
paneled walls

        Or not.

Unseen

How alone the dead remain,
said a poet who now knows
more about the matter.

Pictures and memories,
jotted notes,
planted trees,
carved headstones.
None can halt the degradation
      and fading.

But look in the mirror
and here there are, visible or not,
mother's eyebrows, arcs of steady triumphs,
father's chin, razor sharp grit,
grandma's sweet and sour dimples,
auntie's ovarian cancer.

If you lie down, quiet, you can hear
them running through your veins,
they and their predecessors,
the unknown ones, who invented
the words with which we love.

Flow of the liquid universe,
expanding stars,
sun that hyperboles
our skin while traversing
 toward the black hole.

And we take for granted the drum
of the traffic and the hard steps,
our own drum buried under our garb,
 armor, formal, or casual.

And life goes the way of eggs sunny side up,
or *huevos estrellados*, in Spanish,
 which means both starry and crashed.

Partition of the Waters

I follow the river trail.
Floating memories of charged happiness
reachable by hand, like side road daffodils.
Then I end up by the ocean.

I can't take it whole with my sight: the tempested sea,
its swinging moods, retorting snaps
of foam, grey as liquid rock,
partisan as separate beds, as moving trucks.

I travel north to embrace the roar of a vertical offering
of fresh water, the falls around me
turning upside down what I knew about power;
not an outburst, but an unrelenting outpour
in a surrounding horizon my eyes can exult and rest on.

Almost a miracle.

Celebration

I wish you
a day with a grand finale
and sweet flavors that remind you of your mother's baking.

Slide downhill
on the white and slippery creamy substance.
Climb the indulgent structure that dissolves in your mouth

like a kiss memory,
and then lick your name, the frosting cover,
and the benevolent blue message left there for you.

Ghost that blows
the candles until the room is inhabited
by the smell of burned time. You say your rehearsed words

with the ease
of the third vodka,
with the second wind of the insomniac that refused

to count sheep,
that pulled the wool
over his own eyes. The first name in your outgoing calls list,

I am the gone wolf that haunts you.

Sett Patterns

Rocks don't cry;
removed
from the belly of the earth,
they resist rain
and accept memories.

A misplaced rock
confronted rainy-afternoon,
non-motorized scooter,
and an altered version of myself
flipped and flew downhill,
street performer
on a sett road.

    The dance of the fallen
    angels, stars, coins.

Grit in the eye,
gravel under skinned knee,
pebble in the shoe.

    The banquet of raw,
    rock oysters on a bed of lemons.

Look, Fate, no hands,
says the rookie before
falling out of grace,
running out of options,
sweating the small stuff,
growing gallstones,
biting the dust.

Inkception

Inside the cabin
pressurized like ink on the space pen
I once got as a Christmas present
and allowed me to write lying down
        the white ceiling a canvas
        for the ongoing movies inside my head
        a nonstop gif before they were invented
        or I had seen one   at least.

Now that I think of it
the movie theaters of my equatorial
childhood showed continuous reruns
        over-sized gifs with foreign voices
        that took me places I had only seen
        in books and magazines
        a sea of empty seats around me.

These chambers
have propelled me across oceans
toward places with foreign voices
        the sky a canvas
        for the lands I write as we pass by
        and capture the day before our time
        a sea of full seats around me.

Still in my bag
this pen's pressurized ink
has taken me places I have not seen
in books or magazines.
       Places I find when I stop looking.

Coalescence

Stretch my canvased back
to the yellow paint-brushes of the morning

let sweat overtake the pores on the path
under sycamores and lindens

scream and hear it
over the shower's hollow downpour

watch rhododendrons cast their mauve name
on a fence visible from my bathroom window

bake handmade scones from a recipe in Japanese
in a place that is not a desert

forget the umbrella today
and remember to take it tomorrow

visit the old house still standing
between a dream and the corner shop

step into a room so knitted with cobwebs
that mind blowing doesn't disperse them

come out to a sunny June day
right in front of the ice cream truck

ask for directions
and receive a Chinese ink drawing

find the missing bookmark (the one made of lace)
in *The Aleph* on the night stand

whisper in the spine
that holds the words together

Memory tattoos, happiness,
if you think about it; a stitch work.

Along the Ocean

I drive on the coastal highway,
windows open, South Pacific wind battering my face,
wearing aviator shades but resigned to solid ground.

The sea foams its rage against the *farallón*
while I keep my distance.

The sky turns
the color of a stone wall with lead inlays.
Heavy rock rattles my phone and mixes with the downpour,
hard drums, relentless,
as if the wall is coming down.

I pass by desolated villages,
their everyday routines flooded.
Straw hats hang from kiosks' frames,
blurred out of place and out of time.

Trays with coconut sweets,
cocadas and *melcochas*
on tables covered with plastic tablecloths,
tucked in.
The memory of their flavors assault my palate
but nobody is there to sell.

A few fisher boats lie
on the rain-blackened sand,
their nets spread around them,
gigantic manta rays
against the gray backdrop of the horizon.

I wonder if there are fishermen
trapped by the storm, lost,
their boats barely treading.

I realize that nobody is on the shore
waiting, searching the sea.
There is no danger, I tell myself.
There is no danger.

Notes

Ice Love was written after a presentation by arts educator and artist Dr. Alice Fox. The presentation included a video of the performance depicted in the poem. Event organized by the British Council of Singapore, 2017.

Coalescence was rewritten after seeing the installation *The Exquisite Pirate: Odyssey*, and having a brief conversation with the artist, Sally Smart. The piece is a collage made of fabric, hair, metal and wood. Exhibited at the Singapore Art Museum in 2016.

Acknowledgments

Warm thanks to the editors of the publications in which the following poems first appeared, sometimes in slightly different versions:

Anapest: "Hanging On," "Undertones," and "Thirst"

Bunbury: "Looking Up"

erbace: "Density"

Five 2 One: "Celebration"

Ink Sweat and Tears: "The Angel in My Cupboard"

Octavius Magazine: "Insomnia" and "You Again"

Peeking Cat Poetry Magazine: "Passing by Some Minor Ruins on Our Way to Chichen Itza"

Poetry Quarterly: "Sound Proof"

Taxicab: "Street Art"

The Acentos Review: "*En la Ruta del Mar*" (Version in Spanish of "Along the Ocean Road") and "Staycation"

Three Line Poetry: "Portrait"

The Anthology *Poems to Keep* published "Ice Love" and "Sett Patterns." "Sett Patterns won Third Prize in the 2017 Brian Dempsey Memorial Poetry Competition (Surrey, England)

The Anthology *Warriors with Wings* republished "The Angel in My Cupboard" and "Street Art"

Harbinger Asylum republished "Sound Proof"

My heartfelt gratitude to

Everyone who helped shape this work with their encouragement, reading and critiquing, and overall support.

Rubie, Kristen, Summer, Nicholas, and the whole team at Unsolicited Press, for giving this collection a chance to find its way into the wider world.

Writer and editor Elizabeth Colen, for her insightful comments and suggestions for this work.

Writer and educator Sue Guiney, founder of Writing Through, for her workshops, our conversations about poetry, and for the opportunity to offer creative writing workshops to young people in Cambodia.

My friends at the Singapore Writers Group, a space that fosters creativity and commitment to the craft of writing, with a special nod to its founder, writer Alice Clark-Platts.

My friends at the Writers Group of the AWA Singapore. I treasure our many writing sessions, text exchanges and valuable feedback at the Book Café in River Valley. Many of these poems were born there.

My friends from several virtual poetry groups, the Modern Poetry group in particular. We support one another.

My parents, Lucio (+) and Eugenia; my siblings, María Elena, Salvador, and Priscila, for your love and encouragement.

Roque Darío and Gabriela, mi children, for existing. For your thoughtful feedback to my poems and to many other life projects. You inspire me every day.

Roque Damacela, my life partner, my most trusted reader and generous commenter. Thanks for your love and support. None of this would be possible without you.

About the Author

Lucía Orellana Damacela is the author of *Life Lines* (The Talbot-Heindl Experience, 2018), winner of The Bitchin' Kitsch Chapbook Competition. Her poetry and prose have been published in both English and Spanish in over a dozen countries. Some of the venues featuring Lucía's poetry are *Tin House Online, Cha: An Asian Literary Journal, Sharkpack Annual, Into the Void*, and *The Acentos Review*.

Born in Ecuador, Lucía has lived in North America, Europe, and Asia for many years. Lucía was the recipient of a Fulbright scholarship and holds a PhD in Social Psychology from Loyola University Chicago. She tweets as @lucyda and blogs about her writing at notesfromlucia.wordpress.com.

About the Press

Unsolicited Press was founded in 2012. The press strives to produce outstanding works of fiction, poetry, and nonfiction. Learn more at unsolicitedpress.com.

www.ingramcontent.com/pod-product-compliance
Lightning Source LLC
Chambersburg PA
CBHW030133100526
44591CB00009B/633